E-MAILS FROM SCHEHERAZAD

University of Central Florida Contemporary Poetry Series

Florida A&M University, Tallahassee
Florida Atlantic University, Boca Raton
Florida Gulf Coast University, Ft. Myers
Florida International University, Miami
Florida State University, Tallahassee
University of Central Florida, Orlando
University of Florida, Gainesville
University of North Florida, Jacksonville
University of South Florida, Tampa
University of West Florida, Pensacola

E-MAILS
FROM
SCHEHERAZAD

Mohja Kahf

UNIVERSITY PRESS OF FLORIDA

Gainesville
Tallahassee
Tampa
Boca Raton
Pensacola
Orlando
Miami
Jacksonville
Ft. Myers

Copyright 2003 by Mohja Kahf
Printed in the United States of America on recycled, acid-free paper
All rights reserved

08 07 06 05 04 03 c 6 5 4 3 2 1
08 07   p 6 5 4 3

LIBRARY OF CONGRESS CATALOGING-IN-PUBLICATION DATA
Kahf, Mohja, 1967–
E-mails from Scheherazad / Mohja Kahf.
p. cm. —(The University of Central Florida contemporary
poetry series)
ISBN 0-8130-2620-2 (cloth : alk. paper)
ISBN 0-8130-2621-0 (pbk. : alk. paper)
1. Arab American women—Poetry. 2. Muslim women—Poetry.
3. Women—Poetry. I. Title. II. Contemporary poetry series
(Orlando, Fla.)
PS3611.A66E43 2003
811'.6—dc21   2002043031

Paperback cover photos by Mohja Kahf.

Charcoal drawing of author by Victor Sadovoy.

The University Press of Florida is the scholarly publishing
agency for the State University System of Florida, comprising
Florida A&M University, Florida Atlantic University, Florida
Gulf Coast University, Florida International University, Florida
State University, University of Central Florida, University
of Florida, University of North Florida, University
of South Florida, and University of West Florida.

University Press of Florida
15 Northwest 15th Street
Gainesville, FL 32611–2079
http://www.upf.com

To Najib, Weyam, and Banah,
with screams of delight.

Contents

Acknowledgments   ix

Voyager Dust   1
The Skaff Mother Tells the Story   2
Word from the Younger Skaff   4
Fayetteville as in Fate   6
The Roc   8
The Cherries   11
The Dream of Return   15
The Passing There   18
Lateefa   21
Hijab Scene #3   25
My Grandmother Washes Her Feet in the Sink of the Bathroom
   at Sears   26
I Can Scent an Arab Man a Mile Away   29
Hijab Scene #5   31
My Babysitter Wears a Face-Veil   32
From the Patios of the Alhambra   34
Mahmud's First Letter Home from Minneapolis   36
Descent into JFK   37
Hijab Scene #7   39
Move Over   40
Hijab Scene #1   41
Hijab Scene #2   42
E-mail from Scheherazad   43
So You Think You Know Scheherazad   44
Finding Poems for My Students   46
You Are My Yemen   48
Grandfather   50
The Marvelous Women   51

The Quiet Knight 54

The Woman Dear to Herself 55

To My Queenly Daughters 57

My Body Is Not Your Battleground 58

Sacred Immorality 60

Men Kill Me 61

Ishtar Awakens in Chicago 62

Thawrah des Odalisques at the Matisse Retrospective 64

If the Odalisques 70

Copulation in English 71

The Pistols of Emir Abdel Qader 73

Disbeliever 75

Parturition 1999 77

Snowfall on the Colossal Ruins 79

Khidr's Riddle 81

We Will Continue Like Twin Towers 83

The Fires Have Begun 84

Fatima Migrates in October 85

Redwoods 88

Poem to My Prodigal Brother 89

Would That I Had Met You in Amman 91

Affirmative Action Sonnet 92

Jasmine Snowfall 93

The Fork in the Road 96

Learning to Pray All Over 99

Glossary 101

Acknowledgments

Many of these poems grew out of conversations among the marvelous women of the e-mail salon we began in the summer of 1995, for which I am grateful. I thank Barbara Nimri Aziz of Pacifica Radio–New York for being the first to give me the best kind of encouragement a poet can get and for lending me the ears of her intelligent listenership. I have loving appreciation of Brenda Moossy, Ginny Masullo, Abd al-Hayy and Malika Moore, Lisa Suhair Majaj, Steve Holst, Orlis Wheeler, Barbara Jaquish, Bill Flanagan, and many others for building communities of creativity and heart where I have been lucky to live. A thousand and one thanks to Rahat Kurd for reading the manuscript, an incredibly generous and spontaneous gift of her time and spirit. To Z., my abiding gratitude for the poetry and music of extraordinary friendship.

I am grateful to my editors at the University Press of Florida for their patience and guidance.

This collection includes poems written in the 1980s and the 1990s, as well as recent work. "Grandfather" (1983) is the earliest poem.

I am grateful to the following publications for publishing these poems or earlier versions of them:

Aljadid: "Disbeliever" (1998).

Banipal: "To My Queenly Daughters" (2001), "Men Kill Me," "Ishtar Appears in Chicago" (1999).

A Different Path, ed. Leila Diab and D. H. Melhem: "From the Patios of the Alhambra" (2000).

Exquisite Corpse: "Move Over," "From the Patios of the Alhambra" (1992).

Fellowship: "A Woman Dear to Herself" (1996).

Ivri-Nasawi Poetry Anthology (on-line): "Snowfall on the Colossal Ruins," "Learning to Pray All Over" (2001).

Journal of New Jersey Poets: "Fayetteville as in Fate," "The Dream of Return" (2000).

Jusoor: "If the Odalisques," "*Thawrah des* Odalisques at the Matisse Retrospective" (1996).

Middle East Report: "*Hijab* Scene #7" (1997).

Mizna: "Mahmud Writes His First Letter Home from Minneapolis," "Redwoods" (2001).

The Muslim World: "The Marvelous Women" (2001).

Paris Review: "Copulation in English" (2002).

Paterson Literary Review: "Voyager Dust," "The Roc," "My Grandmother Washes Her Feet in the Sink of the Bathroom at Sears" (2000).

The Poetry of Arab Women, ed. Nathalie Handal: "The Roc" (2001).

Post-Gibran: New Arab-American Writing, ed. Khaled Mattawa and Munir Akash: "My Body Is Not Your Battleground" (1999).

The Space Between Our Footsteps, ed. Naomi Shihab Nye: "Grandfather," "You Are My Yemen" (1998).

Visions International: "Lateefa" (1992).

A glossary of Arabic and French terms and phrases has been provided at the end of the book, at the publisher's behest.

E-MAILS FROM SCHEHERAZAD

Voyager Dust

When they arrive in the new country,
voyagers carry it on their shoulders,
the dusting of the sky they left behind
The woman on the bus in the downy sweater,
I could smell it in her clothes
It was voyager's dust from China
It lay in the foreign stitching of her placket
It said: *We will meet again in Beijing,*
in Guangzhou. We will meet again.
My mother had voyager's dust in her scarves
I imagine her a new student like this woman on the bus,
getting home, shaking out the clothes from her suitcase,
hanging up, one by one, the garments from the old country
On washing day my mother would unroll her scarves
She'd hold one end, my brother or I the other,
and we'd stretch the wet georgette and shake it out
We'd dash, my brother or I, under the canopy,
its soft spray on our faces like the ash
of debris after the destruction of a city,
its citizens driven out across the earth.
We never knew
it was voyager dust. It said:
We will meet again in Damascus,
in Aleppo. We will meet again.
It was Syria in her scarves.
We never knew it
Now it is on our shoulders too

1999

The Skaff Mother Tells the Story

Word came. I had barely time to wrap a bundle
For them: my mincemeat pies, a scarf of wool.
Their father gave them golden liras to survive.
That night, their cousin smuggled them away.
The *Safar Barlik* had begun—the Balkan War—
And the Turks were conscripting all our boys,

Wasting their lives. We wanted them to live, our boys.
Turks stormed our homes, bayoneted the bundled
Carpets to find the hidden sons, take them to war.
The cousin knew a merchant who exported wool
And had a ship in port. They hid and sailed away,
Not even knowing where, our two sons. "Survive,"

I whispered in their ears the night they left, "Survive
And come back to us." We wanted life for our boys
So desperately we didn't think to ask how far away
The ship was bound. "Come home to share the bundle
Of mother, father, kin, house, bread, and wool,"
Was as far as our thinking went. The end of war

Brought cholera that took their father. Where now were
My sons, I wondered, are they cared for, have they survived
The sea, the tides of life, these years? The wool,
I've spun forty years' worth since then. My boys,
I hear, got to Brazil. There they untied the bundle
Of their journey. Faint echo of them finds a way

To us as if through fog. They were too far away
For passage back. Sold off the liras. Had no more wares,
Nor skills to make a living. Their lives' small bundle
Must have wasted smaller. Word stopped. We survived

On scraps, rumors passed across the ocean about my boys,
Grown into men and married. I don't know if I will

See them again in life. Have they found wool
To keep them warm in their new land? We sent them away,
I swear, to keep them with us; they were only boys.
Fourteen and fifteen is too young to suffer war
And maybe die. But what is it to survive
Like grafts cut off a tree, a child without a bundle?

The wool of my heart is threadbare after the years and wars
And I keep in a bundle the names of my lost boys
Survive, we told them, and sent them unthinkably away

2001

Word from the Younger Skaff

I was still hungry
when I left home, mother,
to disappear from the one piece
of earth I knew. The Ottoman liras
father gave us and the mincemeat pies
you wrapped in a woolen bundle
were everything I and my brother
had from home. They had to last
a lifetime. I was fourteen
the night we left, and
it was dinnertime.

Yumma, that hunger's never left me,
even though I'm big as an ox,
fifty-five now, married,
and master of a house
with a good larder.
Hunger still lurches
inside me, like the sea voyage
from Beirut to Brazil.
Sometimes I think
I could eat the house out,
hearth, oven, gate, and all.

My little girl knows how
to make your mincemeat pies,
folded in neat, small triangles.
I described them to her and we mixed
flour and yeast in different measures,
laughing at the failures, till we got it.
I could never teach her mother.
My wife was a good woman,

but like you, cooked only dishes
she'd learned from her own *avó.*

Wherever you are, O *mãe,*
I bet it fills your belly to know
there's a twelve-year-old Brazilian girl
with your hair and eyes, who,
though she's never seen
you or your kitchen fire, makes
Syrian meat pies proper,
baked golden and sealed
with your same thumbpress,
precise as an Ottoman coin.

2001

Fayetteville as in Fate

When I moved to Fayetteville, Arkansas
I soon learned to say it Fay'tteville, as in fate
I came into town the American way,
the immigrant way, the upwardly mobile
bedouin trekking across the highway
I moved here from New Jersey and I like it just fine,
although I miss belligerent store clerks
and being able to rent *Abi Fawq el-Shagara*
at the Egyptian video/pizzeria/travel agency/
check cashing service/grocery store
I miss practicing my Urdu with random gas station attendants,
although once a Wal-Mart associate here told me *"Shukran"*
and turned out to have known the Nile
That's fate

It is Fay'tteville as in fate:
There is Cherokee and Choctaw in it,
around the rims of people's eyes
There is Spain and France left in the names of things
There is Wild West and Old South here
Sometimes the music of the Ozarks
spills down the mountainside
and it is green and brown, and I think I hear it

I hear that people pick "poke" here
and my family memory stirs with people
who picked the wild herbs, the *khibbezé*, of other mountains
Whole populations of seed sowers and herb knowers
some from Damascus, some from Fayetteville, they meet
in my head like the walls of the Red Sea crashing together
I roll dizzily toward them
like the bowling ball of a very bad bowler

I mix metaphors among them
like a reckless cook throwing things into a pot,
hoping they don't explode when they touch each other,
hoping they don't turn bitter when the heat rises

Their names and their languages are wildly different
and they believe improbable, vile things about each other
But see the turn of wrist when a woman from here
or a woman from there kneads dough
Although the bread will be twisted
into different shapes for baking,
the hands move with a similar knowledge
See how a farmer takes up a handful of dirt
This one wears overalls and that one wears a *sirwal*,
but the open hand with the dirt in its creases
makes a map both can read

But who will coax them close enough to know this?
Darling, it is poetry
Darling, I am a poet
It is my fate
like this, like this, to kiss
the creases around the eyes and the eyes
that they may recognize each other:

> *May their children e-mail one another and not bomb one another*
> *May they download each other's mother's bread recipes*
> *May they sell yams and yogurts to each other at a conscionable profit*
> *May they learn each other's tongue and put words into each other's mouth*

> Say *Amen*
> Say آمـيـن
> Say it, say it

1995

The Roc

Here's my mom and dad leaving
Damascus, the streets they knew,
the familiar shape of food, the daily
boiling and cooling of fresh milk,
the measurement of time by mosque sounds,
the scrape of heavy wooden shutters. Anyone
back home who had no phone fell off
the disc of their new world: tomato-cart man,
Crazy Fat'na the Goatwoman,
all the gatekeepers at the door
they left behind

Here they are crossing the world,
hoisting up all they know like a sail,
landing in Utah. March, 1971.
They know nothing
about America: how to grocery
shop or open a bank account,
how the milk comes, thin
glass bottles chinking tin,
what "you bet" or "sure thing" meant
in real spoken English, outside
their London grammar books so creased,
so carefully underlined. It was,
my mother said, as if a monstrous bird
had seized them up and dropped them
in a fantastic, lunar terrain

Here's my mother studying
the instructions on the coin-
box of a laundry machine,
enrolling us in kindergarten,

tape-recording her college lectures so
she could play, replay, decode
the stream of alien phonemes into words
There she is refolding foil, stretching
the little budget over the month, making
the ten-cent toys our treasures
of Sinbad

    Here's my father staking his life's
savings on one semester in grad school
He works hard, does well in class,
and on the day before the last dollar
of the life savings is gone, with rent due
and America costing more than he dreamed,
more than can be saved in a Syrian lifetime,
he walks into the department chair's office
and the chair gives him a job teaching
Other friendly natives explain coupons,
student housing, how not to pay retail,
and help my parents find bargain-basement
merchandise

    The pilgrims were so happy at surviving
that first semester in the new world,
they had a feast. That's mom
laughing at the strange loaf of the bread
There's dad holding up the new world coffee
in its funny striped boxes. That's us,
small, weightless, wobbly with the vertigo
of the newly landed
voyager

Here they are, mom and dad, telephoning
back home, where the folks gather around
the transmission as if it came from the moon.
The phone call to Syria was for epic
events only. The line pulsates
with the beating of enormous wings.
They shout and shout into the receiver
as if the other end was a thousand and one
ages away. Spiny talon
digs into rock.

1998

The Cherries

I left Syria many years ago, as a child,
and I don't remember Syria
but Syria remembers me:
I am sure of it

Syria keeps a small pillow
embroidered with my name
Syria is saving some cherries
in a bowl for me
at the back of the refrigerator

Last April, a friend just back from Syria
phoned to say he'd tried to buy a book of poetry
in a small bookshop in Srujeh,
a book wedged high on a dusty shelf
The shopkeeper said,
"You can't have any from that stack;
they're for Mohja, daughter
of Monzer and Maysoon."
See? Syria still remembers
its children who live in late capitalism,
an information age away

Some people say that Syria
would stare at me with provincial hostility
if I went back
Some people say all Syria would do
is empty my wallet with demands for bribes,
complain about the price of melons,
calculate the value of my watch and ring,
and turn me in to the state police

I am sure that if I went back to Syria,
there would be music
and all the melodrama of a Hindi movie:
The ground would love me
The trees would lean toward me like aunts
The mountains would protect me like cousins
The ancient churches would kiss my forehead
The mosques would hold and rock me in their arches
The synagogues would lay blessings on my shoulders like a shawl

I am sure the fountains would splash my feet with water
like playmates who've known me since first grade
Every morning would smell like coffee and cardamom
Every afternoon would taste like coriander and mint
Every evening would linger like the music of the oud
We would all stretch out on the roof under the stars,
eating nuts and drinking tea in small flowered glasses

I am sure Damascus would puff on a nargileh
and laugh a deep laugh like a granduncle
Aleppo would croon for me
like a handsome blue-eyed muezzin
Hama would frown and act stern
but with a secret kindness on its brow
Homs would set oval platters before me
of stuffed eggplants spilling over with almonds,
and Latakia would take me to the beach
and skip with me and buy me big bright plastic balls

I am sure the villages would soak my hair in henna
and lead me to their daughter's wedding in Deir al-Zawr
The gypsies would tie sashes around my hips
and play their squeaky violins and whirl me
The Circassians would send a gorgeous bridegroom

to carry me away in dark of night on jet-black horses
caparisoned and tasseled red and gold
The Kurds would pierce my ears with silver Kurdish words
Syria's Palestinians would embroider me a dress
and tie my schoolbooks in a satchel
The Druze would introduce me to esoteric mysteries
in small white mountaintop temples
The Alawites would sit me down and tell me
old and powerful stories, handed down
in hushed voices by a hundred generations

Hatreds based on class and sect would disappear,
along with political prisons and electric torture-prods,
and no one would be afraid to be seen talking to each other
or listening to poetry about Syria
(This is my poem and I can do what I want
with the world in it)

I can picture such things because all these years
I have traced those people and places on my map
See, here on my map of Syria

It's faded where it's been folded
because I carry it in a pocket called heart
(Look, I told you this was melodrama)
Here's how the soap opera goes: Syria
plays a poor woman with a cruel master
who wouldn't let her care for me
as a child deserves to be cared for
He wouldn't let her feed me cherries
and dress me in Aleppan wool
He wouldn't let her pin little gold trinkets on me
to protect me from the evil eye
So she had to send her child far away

even though I cried and she cried
(How do these Egyptian movies ever end?)

And where did I go?
And what did I become?
And in my new home did I eat cherries?
And in my adopted family was I warm like Aleppan wool?
What happens to a child who can no longer speak
the language of its mother?
What happens to a bird when it can no longer fly
in its natural habitat?
What happens to a girl who wanted once to put her head
on a small pillow embroidered with her name?

Tell me who ate the cherries
They were in a small bowl in the back of the refrigerator
They were for me because Syria remembers
I was
sure of it

1998

The Dream of Return

I.

It's October and she's turning
thirty, holding out her arm
like a branch, turning the green
leaf over, finding its veins of gold,
its shocking bloodred patterns.

She is driving through the ancient city
to taste the meat of the walnut.
What is the riddle of father and mother?
What was the shell of knowledge
that encased her on the day of her birth?

II.

This is the merchant's family
in the old quarter of the city.
This is the price of the oil
we rub on the infant's head and belly.
This is the woolen carpet

silencing the footfall of mother.
Here are father's small cups
on the beaten copper tray.
The hush means his elder
half sisters are visiting.

The youngest children line
around the table, ready
to greet father and guests. Hear
the pious murmurings of the aunts
drip into the white stone fountain.

Have we opened the vein yet?
Maybe it is the green tracery
of shade across the inner garden,
the atrium of the house,
where father bubbles a water pipe.

Smoke that curls from his nostrils
writes stories that will hang
in the air for fifty years.
These are the crossed arms
of mother, her voice

shrilling up the stairwell spiral,
the deep well at the center of the house.
Laxness and shirking make her angry.
The adult sons are in their chamber,
creating a work ethic out of her anger.

III.

The sons journey, work hard, marry
women of unacceptable houses,
never return. The old parents die.
All the woolen carpets are rolled up.
Grandchildren are born far away

speaking different languages,
never knowing each other.
They drive through new cities
in the four directions,
but the tracery of gold

remains in the belly of their hands.
One day a granddaughter turns thirty
in October, like a leaf turning gold,
falling from a tree in the four winds.
She drives into an old, old city.

She puts a key she didn't know she had
into a door and it fits.
There is the uneven sound
of a walnut rolling. There are oil stains
shaped like infant memory.

She sees the mother's reproaches
lying where they were flung,
hard and small. She sees curlicued
stories hanging in the air like dust.
She lifts up a sheet.

These are the very cups
on the copper tray.
This is the rim marked red
with remembrance, horror, love,
her own blood filling
this deep well

1997

The Passing There

My brother and I crossed through a field.
Soybeans grew there. We were nine and ten.
It wasn't ours. It was golden.
I remember raspberry bushes
way at the back, and rusted wire,
once a fence, defunct now and trampled under

by generations of children who belonged
to this Indiana landscape in the seventies,
sixties, forties, tens: Matthews and Deborahs,
Toms and Betsys, Wills and Dots. Here we were,
Yaman and Mohja,
getting a kajillion scratches,
knuckles bleeding, on our little knees,
forgetting everything but gold and green,
scrabbling for another sweet hit of summer berry.

The man who owned the field was no Robert Frost
although he spoke colloquial. "Git
off my property," he shouted, "Or I'll—"
The rest of what he said I do not care
to repeat. It expressed his concerns
about our religion and ethnic origin.
He had a rifle. We went on home.

My brother knows this song: running home,
behind us, a field that wasn't ours,
ahead, a house of alien expectations,
the cruel kindnesses of parents who,
coming from the Syrian sixties,
thought they had succeeded

in growing little hothouse Syrians.
My brother and I crossed through a field;

we ran and ran. Somewhere in Syria,
earth brown like nut, sky like the turquoise
in my earring, other purples waited,
a plum tree had our name on it. Days passed
in another country, like photographs
with our silhouettes cut out, where one day
we would fit back in, we thought.

There the vineyard watchman chased away
children whose names he knew, yelling at them
in the language of their parents
and their parents' parents,
our parallel-universe Syrian selves among them,
hearing their names called among the others,
Yaman and Mohja, running home
and getting there, skin bright, panting,
getting home.

My brother and I crossed through a field.
Its golden music wasn't ours. We listened
to its cornflower choirs and tried
to feel like Hoosiers. Aunts and uncles
fed us Syrian pastries, heavily syruped,
and parents promised Arabian gold.
We sang the anthems
of their remembered landscapes on request
for visitors and foreign guests.
At school, we pledged allegiance,
trying not to feel like traitors.

My brother knows this song:
How we have been running
to leap the gulch between two worlds, each
with its claim. Impossible for us
to choose one over the other,
and the passing there
makes all the difference.

2001

Lateefa

Connie, Connie!
Constance Mustafa's
marrying Muhammad Smith
down in Bayonne Park today
Then they'll leave from Journal Square
and we will have come full circle
God, I love this state!
Standing there with its hip thrust out

the way a woman does when she's holding a baby
with her left arm and with her right
heaping chicken and Hungarian potato salad
onto a paper plate and at the same time calling
*"Lateefa, help your brother with that soda
before he spills it all over himse—Lateefa!"*
then glancing—before the whole thing separates
into component parts: baby, paper plate, chicken,
brother, Lateefa, soda, the Hungarian
potato salad, and the woman cleaning up the mess—
glancing with frustration and desire at the volleyball game
commencing across the park
Connie, Connie! This is it!
a zoom lens into the twenty-first century:
An Afro-Caribbean Muslim woman
eating paprika-tossed Hungarian potato
salad at the wedding of a Pakistani-American to a West Indian man
Be happy, Columbus: At last, at least
the two Indies meet. In Jersey, in Jersey City.
(Oh, the Hungarian is from her mother's side.)

It's New Jersey does it, Connie
It's the Nile and the Euphrates

pouring into Passaic Valley, into the Raritan River
swelling it up sometimes in the spring so the crushed
cigarette packs and Styrofoam cups from Johnson Park
are swept into its eddies, grabbed and dropped
by cawing gulls.
I was born here—BORN!
INNA YOU-ESS-AY—oh Bruce,
oh Connie, I
got nowhere to go back to

> *(Daddy, you can talk to me*
> *all you want about Palestine*
> *And I'll be faithful to the end*
> *but I don't know it, never*
> *smelled its rainwet streets, don't know*
> *its stoops and backyards and chicken coops*
> *and those neighbors standing beside that old Ford*
> *in the black & white photograph. My Aunt Cauthar,*
> *Daddy, I love her—I think of cougar,*
> *sleek, black-haired, and courageous—*
> *but I don't know her, or the abundant rivers*
> *of what she really means)*

I know New Jersey. I've run
my fingers up and down its spine,
scaled the vertebrae of official buildings
on Broad Street, in Newark,
taken Uncle Ali to Immigration.
I know where the Sister Clara Muhammad Schools,
white *kufis* and black *khimars* bobbing, hold their fairs,
and where the Ansar Allah
peddle Islam in little vials
of odiferous oils, sir,
to dubious passers-by

I know like uncles the bearded immigrant shaikhs,
cringed as they've stammered into microphones,
trying to amend
the miscommunication of a thousand some-odd years
in one thirteen-second sound bite at 6:08 P.M.
I've visited the gated suburban developments where
upwardly mobile Egyptian teenagers lose their *shib-shibs,*
heard Qawwali music spiral up condominium stairwells
and twirl over the heads of the great-great-great-grandchildren
of Leif Eriksson and Akbar and Zobaidah and Son-Jara
as they play and slide together and tumble into each other

I know the storefront mosques in the neighborhoods
where *"Allahu akbar"* alternates
with *"doo-wop, she-boom, she-boom,"*
where church bells often ring at sunset,
confusing us in Ramadan
New Jersey slings us all across that hip,
that hip thrust out, and hopes to manage
Connie Mustafa won't change her name
when she marries Muhammad Smith
And we will teach Omar the Great
at Roosevelt Elementary

Hey, Connie, you think we can do it?
If we love what we are we can make it
survive here: George Washington, meet
Harun al-Rashid. *She-boom, she-boom.*
Already, here's Abigail Abdullah,
Pilgrim-to-Mecca's Progress to Jersey City,
marrying Miles Ali Standish
(*Want to make something of it?*
Want to sue, want to issue a ticket?)
Connie, there's room here for all of us

I believe that. And if we love
the freedom we've found here,
we can give it a fresh—

> "—yeah, a fresh cup of soda, Lateefa.
> Hold the cup for your brother, help me pour it.
> Lateefa, help your brother before he spill—!"

"Officer, if you could just wait for the wedding to—"

**"What wedding, lady? I don't see no priest.
Where's the priest?"**

"We don't have—see, we aren't—we're—"

**"Lady, you people gotta move your cars or they get
tickets, see?"**

"But Connie's getting—this is a wedding! Just wait one sec
till the ceremony—"

"Lady, move these cars or I give them tickets.

"But, Officer—"

"Lady—!"

> "*LATEEFA!*"

1990

Hijab Scene #3

"Would you like to join the PTA?" she asked,
tapping her clipboard with her pen.
"I would," I said, but it was no good,
she wasn't seeing me.
"Would you like to join the PTA?" she repeated.
"I would," I said,
but I could've been antimatter.
A regular American mother next to me
shrugged and shook her head.
"I would, I would," I sent up flares,
beat on drums, waved navy flags,
tried smoke signals, American Sign Language,
Morse code, Western Union, telex, fax,
Lt. Uhura tried hailing her
for me on another frequency.
"Dammit, Jim, I'm a Muslim woman, not a Klingon!"
—but the positronic force field of hijab
jammed all her cosmic coordinates.
Can we save the ship we're both on,
can we save
the dilithium crystals?

1993

My Grandmother Washes Her Feet
in the Sink of the Bathroom at Sears

My grandmother puts her feet in the sink
    of the bathroom at Sears
to wash them in the ritual washing for prayer,
wudu,
because she has to pray in the store or miss
the mandatory prayer time for Muslims
She does it with great poise, balancing
herself with one plump matronly arm
against the automated hot-air hand dryer,
after having removed her support knee-highs
and laid them aside, folded in thirds,
and given me her purse and her packages to hold
so she can accomplish this august ritual
and get back to the ritual of shopping for housewares

Respectable Sears matrons shake their heads and frown
as they notice what my grandmother is doing,
an affront to American porcelain,
a contamination of American Standards
by something foreign and unhygienic
requiring civic action and possible use of disinfectant spray
They fluster about and flutter their hands and I can see
a clash of civilizations brewing in the Sears bathroom

My grandmother, though she speaks no English,
catches their meaning and her look in the mirror says,
I have washed my feet over Iznik tile in Istanbul
with water from the world's ancient irrigation systems
I have washed my feet in the bathhouses of Damascus
over painted bowls imported from China

among the best families of Aleppo
And if you Americans knew anything
about civilization and cleanliness,
you'd make wider washbasins, anyway
My grandmother knows one culture—the right one,

as do these matrons of the Middle West. For them,
my grandmother might as well have been squatting
in the mud over a rusty tin in vaguely tropical squalor,
Mexican or Middle Eastern, it doesn't matter which,
when she lifts her well-groomed foot and puts it over the edge.
"You can't do that," one of the women protests,
turning to me, "Tell her she can't do that."
"We wash our feet five times a day,"
my grandmother declares hotly in Arabic.
"My feet are cleaner than their sink.
Worried about their sink, are they? I
should worry about my feet!
My grandmother nudges me, "Go on, tell them."

Standing between the door and the mirror, I can see
at multiple angles, my grandmother and the other shoppers,
all of them decent and goodhearted women, diligent
in cleanliness, grooming, and decorum
Even now my grandmother, not to be rushed,
is delicately drying her pumps with tissues from her purse
For my grandmother always wears well-turned pumps
that match her purse, I think in case someone
from one of the best families of Aleppo
should run into her—here, in front of the Kenmore display

I smile at the midwestern women
as if my grandmother has just said something lovely about them
and shrug at my grandmother as if they
had just apologized through me
No one is fooled, but I

hold the door open for everyone
and we all emerge on the sales floor
and lose ourselves in the great common ground
of housewares on markdown

1991

I Can Scent an Arab Man a Mile Away

    My stubbly-chinned,
black-haired, tawny-skinned
Arab male kin, the white-robed
and the black-tied of them,
milling on the male side of a wedding,
can be counted on for many good things:
    To be politicized about Palestine
from the third grade, at the latest;
to cushion the tumbles of small children
without pausing in conversation;
to sit on the floor, leaning forward,
elbow on one raised knee and eat heartily,
even if the meal is only stale bread
soaked in broth; and to recognize
Scripture and poetry.
    They may be
mustachio'd, macho, patriarchal,
sexist, egotistical, parochial—
They may, as men may,
think themselves indomitable,
being easily manipulable,
—but they're mine, my
sleek and swarthy, hairy-chested,
curly-headed lovers of the Prophet
and lovers of the Virgin,
sons of the city street and village boys,
wanderers tribal and global.

I know them by the rims around their eyes
I know them by the sheen upon their skin
I know them by the growling *ghayns*
and gnawing *dāds* and hoarse hungry *khās*

that rumble up from the hollow in their chests
and fill the throat and swell the cheek,
distend the lips and pearl off the tongue,
and emerge, a language, theirs—ours—mine.
    My men, familiar
as the road home,
the threshold of love
I can leap astride their legendary chivalry,
if I remember
what words will make it carry me
aloft, aloft . . .
    Oh, I know those words
I hold those reins
These fine horses won't,
despite their snorting,
rearing, pacing, bucking,
cavorting, caracoling, won't escape me.

(God, they look so sexy in those checkered scarves.)

1992

Hijab Scene #5

"Assalam-O-alaikum, sister"
"Assalam-O-alaikum, ma'am"
"Assalam-O-alaikum" at the mailbox
"Assalam-O-alaikum" by the bus stop
When you're wearing *hijab,* Black men
you don't even know materialize
all over Hub City
like an army of chivalry,
opening doors, springing
into gallantry.

Drop the scarf, and (if you're light)
you suddenly pass (lonely) for white.

1993

My Babysitter Wears a Face-Veil

My babysitter, Selwa, wears a face-veil
whenever she goes out
She drives her husband's four-by-four
on mountainous truck tires
Only her eyes show,
like the dark parts of Himalayan mountains peeking
through the veiling clouds and snow

She barrels down Livingston Avenue
with the confidence of a teenaged driver,
her children strapped in back
A distinguished gentleman is exiting First Fidelity
Bank—astonished, he pivots! pirouettes!
His suit corners flutter delicately
He becomes for her a businessman ballerina
He can't see
her grin, but she does
A middle-aged woman customer is transfixed, and twirls,
in her Eva Gabor wig, on a stool at The Hungry Peddler
Selwa thinks it's delicious,
whatever she's eating
A young pink-collar worker
on her way to Johnson and Johnson's
in a bright blue Nissan, stops and stares,
bared lipstick in midair
Selwa waves at her gaily

My babysitter steps on the brakes
and the continents grind, shifting
gears: Then henna,
howdahs, saffron, gold embroidery,
and Circassian queens on elephants intersect

with Allied Movers' tractor-trailers, baseball caps,
suction-cup Garfield cats, Calvin Klein
mascara, and a pack of Camels on the dash;
Zuleika meets the Marlboro Man across a delayed green
The secretary-next-door is face-to-face with Laila
Somewhere, songs from *Guys and Dolls* are scrambled
with the soundtrack of *Khali balak min Zuzu* and both
are drowned out by The Monster Truck & Auto
Show-Show-Show of the Century-ree-ree

At intersections do drivers know
each other for a moment?
Is it the lull, the looking in glass,
the lane lines, the language
of light and movement—
Is traffic transcendental?
Do Selwa and the woman with the lipstick
and the trucker see
behind the blind spot for an instant?

When the signal changes, my babysitter
cranks up the elephant-grease
and roars forward on her mount
to learn English, buy milk, get her GED
Just another driver
on the demographic edge of New Jersey

1994

From the Patios of the Alhambra

From the patios of the Alhambra I come
and out of the fountains of the Taj Mahal
Hispano-Arab women sang me in Andalusia, in forgotten
    vernaculars
Palestinian women embroider me into the breastplates
    of dresses
I flow like wine through the *Rubayat* of Omar Khayyam
and like blood through Ibn Sina's *Textbook of Medicine*
I am carved into Baghdadi doorframes and was once
whispered passionately by the concubines of Harun al-Rashid
and still swing on the hips of dancing women
in Khartoum and Cairo and Rawalpindi
I am pried into mosaic mother-of-pearl in old Damascus houses
and hammered into the silver dagger-hilts of Omani chieftains
Caliphs' daughters slung me around their waists, and scribes
in the universities of Samarkand and Bukhara diligently
    copied me
I am in the archives of al-Azhar and the alcoves of Topkapi
and the hammams of Aleppo where the turbaned, half-naked,
told stories in the steam while the *m'kayis* scrubbed them
and I am in the scrub and the clink-clunk
of the wooden bathroom shoes, and all the rhythmic noises
of Aleppo and of the generations
I am in the *shaikhani* dances of Assyrian churchfolk
I pause in the cupped hand of a Kurdish villager
while she considers the surplus of substance or its lack
and I move in her measuring motion
Swahili women weave me into the messages of leso-cloths
and give them to their daughters to be worn on wedding nights
The horsemen of the Tuareq wrap me around their faces
and the *mehndi* painters of India trace me

onto the palms and feet of maidens
Mirrorworkers stitch my irregular circles into velvet vests,
and old women tell me to children: I dazzle!
I am in the drumbeat of the Mandingo
and its echo in the heartbeat of the New World
I am in the work of the Lebanese grocers of Argentina
and the Indian tailors of Trinidad
Also in the designs of rhinestone on denim in Detroit
and pinned haphazardly on the bulletin boards
    of Mizrahi synagogues
and even now being spliced together in video
studios and public-access cable stations
in Chicago and California and Toronto
and peddled by descendents of Khalil Gibran
on the back roads of South Carolina
    I am kohl; I am scented oil; I am spice
    I am rice of every hue
    cooked with nuts, pine and pistachio
    I am a seal of musk, opening, joyous,
    flinging myself, mingling
    with the oils of your body,
    merging with you,
    emerging together in a new medium
        Meeting with ululations the new millennium

1990

Mahmud's First Letter Home from Minneapolis

Dear Mom, I landed in America—
might as well say the moon
The air is a different element
The cars are new and shiny like jewels
The sun is made of another fire
The sky is an alien blue

Jordan's just a speck on the map, Ma—
I said I made it to the moon!
I'm bouncy—no gravity here,
America's got different rules
You should see what the girls wear
over here—but never mind that—
My brother's taking good care of me
and I'm eating, don't worry—
not like our food, but not bad

It's like I'm in a film, but for real.
Everyone speaks English fast,
not a bit like we learned it in school
They wave and say "hi,"
all the folks we know
as my brother and I
motorbike through the glittering night
There's snow. And ice. The music is fine.
And the girls—I love you, Ma!—
My brother sends love—write soon.

1999

Descent into JFK

Descent into New York airspace is hard.
This is no fluffy white dreamfield
for thirteen-year-old schoolgirls anymore
but a tight grid of world tensions
replicated to scale. Languages crisscross
from polyglot to melting pot.
As the cabin pressure changes,
the world shifts its weight
to the other foot. Great care
is required now in opening
the compartments of the mind.
Her Arabic thoughts, ways
of walking, of looking and talking,
wad up like a faded identity card.
Here everyone believes only Israel
is real; the people living in its shadow,
her clan and family, do not exist.
If they saw Uncle Shukri
in his checkered headscarf,
like when he let her ride
behind him on his motorbike,
they'd think he was a terrorist.
They'd never know Khaleda
has a Ph.D.
because she wears a veil they'll
never see beyond.
     "Local temperature 17 degrees."
People reach for coats and caps.
She reaches for protection from the weather
and other kinds of cold, rummages up
lipstick to change the color of her words,

earrings to dangle like her fears,
things that cover and reveal.
    "Arrival time 10:42 P.M."
People synchronize their watches.
She tunes the dials within
for descent into another world.
Other eyes will look at her with other
expectations.
The walkway opens:
This is America.
Who will be waiting?
Who will be descending?

1992

Hijab Scene #7

No, I'm not bald under the scarf
No, I'm not from that country
where women can't drive cars
No, I would not like to defect
I'm already American
But thank you for offering
What else do you need to know
relevant to my buying insurance,
opening a bank account,
reserving a seat on a flight?
Yes, I speak English
Yes, I carry explosives
They're called words
And if you don't get up
Off your assumptions,
They're going to blow you away

1995

Move Over

We are the spreaders of prayer rugs
in highway gas stations at dawn
We are the fasters at company banquets
before sunset in Ramadan
We wear veils and denim,
prayer caps and Cubs caps
as over the prairie to the halal pizzeria
we go. We don't know
what to do at weddings:
wear white and cut the cake?
wear red and receive garlands?
rap songs or tambourines?
It doesn't matter. Enough to have
a pita bread, a carbonated drink,
e-mail to read, and thou
We will intermarry and commingle
and multiply, oh, how we'll multiply
Muhammad-lovers in the motley
miscellany of the land

1990

Hijab Scene #1

"You dress strange," said a tenth-grade boy with bright blue hair
to the new Muslim girl with the headscarf in homeroom,
his tongue-rings clicking on the "tr" in "strange."

1992

Hijab Scene #2

"You people have such restrictive dress for women,"
she said, hobbling away in three-inch heels and panty hose
to finish out another pink-collar temp pool day.

1992

E-mail from Scheherazad

Hi, babe. It's Scheherazad. I'm back
For the millennium and living in Hackensack,
New Jersey. I tell stories for a living.
You ask if there is a living in that.

You must remember: Where I come from,
Words are to die for. I saved the virgins
From beheading by the king, who was killing
Them to still the beast of doubt in him.

I told a story. He began to listen and I found
That story led to story. Powers unleashed, I wound
The thread around the pirn of night. A thousand days
Later, we got divorced. He'd settled down

& wanted a wife & not so much an artist.
I wanted publication. It was hardest,
Strangely, on my sister, Dunyazad. She
Was the one who nightly used to start it.

She and my ex do workshops now in schools
On art & conflict resolution. Narrative rules!
I teach creative writing at Montclair State,
And I'm on my seventh novel and book tour.

Shahrayar and I share custody of our little girl.
We split up amicably. I taught him to heal
His violent streak through stories, after all,
And he helped me uncover my true call.

2000

So You Think You Know Scheherazad

So you think you know Scheherazad
So you think she tells you bedtime stories
that will please and soothe,
invents fairy creatures
who will grant you wishes

Scheherazad invents nothing
Scheherazad awakens
the demons under your bed
They were always there
She locks you in with them

And when you struggle to escape from them,
and when you run
to the very end of the corridor, you find
that it leads only to another corridor
And every door you open is a false door
And suddenly you find yourself in a room
within a room within a room within a room
and suddenly you find yourself forced to meet them,
the demons she unleashes,
the terrors that come from
within you and within her
And suddenly Scheherazad is nowhere to be found
but the stories she unlocked go on and on—

this is the power of the telling of a story—
And suddenly you find yourself
swimming through the sea to the Reef of Extremity,
flying to the Valley of All That Is Possible,
walking barefoot on a blade

over the Chasm of Flames,
landing in a field where you wrestle with Iblis,

whose form changes into your lover,
into Death, into knowledge, into God,
whose face changes into Scheherazad—

And suddenly you find yourself.

2000

Finding Poems for My Students

O my students,
I scour the world of words
to bring you poems like the rocks
my girls dig up in riverbanks
and come running to show me
because the notches in them
say something true, something
that an ancient Wisdom
wanted us to see.

I run to you, pockets full of poems.
I select: This poem will help you pass a test.
Here is one that is no help at all,
but is beautiful; take it, take it.

O my scroungers after merely passing grades,
I bring you poems I have hiked high
and far to find, knowing
they will mostly end up like the rocks
my daughters find, tossed in drawers
with old batteries, mislaid keys,
scraps bearing the addresses
of people whose names
you no longer recognize or need.

Your current glazed-eye indifference
doesn't bother me. One day,
when you are either cleaning house
or moving (and sooner or later
everyone must do one or the other),
you will shake the drawer and the poem

will fall out. And may the poem be for you
the one phone number in the universe
you were looking for, and may it be
for you the mislaid key
to your greatest need.
On that day,
you will read.

2000

You Are My Yemen

"God bless our Yemen and our Damascus."
—Muhammad

You are my Yemen and my Damascus
You are the goal of my winter journey and my summer
You are my city and its streets
You are my village and its fields

I shimmy up palm trees to wait for you
To squint into the sun and watch for you
You are my caravan loaded with lentils and cracked wheat
Snaking its way into town
We the city-dwellers trill with joy
Layla and Majnun will fry chopped onions tonight!

You are my neighborhood and my quarter
My children running through the gate, scattering chickens
My women leaning out of windows shrilling,
"Did you get the bundle I left for you at Um Ahmad's?"
My men bringing crates of ripe vegetables
Buthayna and Jamil will cook eggplants in their rice tonight

You are Joha who appears everywhere
And leaves everyone laughing and gasping
You are the con artist who takes everything
And leaves the smile on the face
Go ahead, trick me out of myself

You are my Yemen and my Damascus
You are my Cairo and my Baghdad
Your arms are Umayyad minarets
Your thighs are Tigris and Euphrates
Your eyelids are Egyptian cinema screens

You know the lines to all the Shadia movies
You know the rhymes of all the hanging odes
Your body moves like the sand dunes of Rub' al-Khali and I
    am lost in it
You know the flavor of the clumps of rice
that cling to the soft seedy insides of fried eggplant

I fly to you, I roam over
my Yemen, my Damascus
in winter, in summer
my village, my city
my minarets, my rivers

I burst through the gates toward you,
my field, my neighbor
The harvest crates, the trays of rice are gathered
Here is the time of fasting, time of feasting
Here is the call to prayer, trill of joy

Here are the long-awaited evenings
Here you are. Here am I.
Your face
the horizon
I want to see

1996

Grandfather

Your grandchildren
are climbing
the oak tree in the backyard
on the planks of wood
you nailed in its side
Soon they will not remember
who spaced them so evenly
Do you feel the weight
of a small foot on your heart,
and when they reach the top
will you grasp their hands
and hoist them up with you?

1983

The Marvelous Women

All women speak two languages:
the language of men
and the language of silent suffering.
Some women speak a third,
the language of queens.
They are marvelous
and they are my friends.

My friends give me poetry.
If it were not for them
I'd be a seamstress out of work.
They send me their dresses
and I sew together poems,
enormous sails for ocean journeys.

My marvelous friends, these women
who are elegant and fix engines,
who teach gynecology and literacy,
and work in jails and sing and sculpt
and paint the ninety-nine names,
who keep each other's secrets
and pass on each other's spirits
like small packets of leavening,

it is from you I fashion poetry.
I scoop up, in handfuls, glittering
sequins that fall from your bodies
as you fall in love, marry, divorce,
get custody, get cats, enter
supreme courts of justice,
argue with God.

You rescuers on galloping steeds
of the weak and the wounded—
Creatures of beauty and passion,
powerful workers in love—
you are the poems.
I am only your stenographer.
I am the hungry transcriber
of the conjuring recipes you hoard
in the chests of your great-grandmothers.

My marvelous friends—the women
of brilliance in my life,
who levitate my daughters,
you are a coat of many colors
in silk tie-dye so gossamer
it can be crumpled in one hand.
You houris, you mermaids, swimmers
in dangerous waters, defiers of sharks—

My marvelous friends,
thirsty Hagars and laughing Sarahs,
you eloquent radio Aishas,
Marys drinking the secret
milkshakes of heaven,
slinky Zuleikas of desire,
gay Walladas, Harriets
parting the sea, Esthers in the palace,
Penelopes of patient scheming,

you are the last hope of the shrinking women.
You are the last hand to the fallen knights
You are the only epics left in the world

Come with me, come with poetry
Jump on this wild chariot, hurry—

Help me with these wayward, snorting horses
Together we will pull across the sky
the sun that will make the earth radiant—

or burn in its terrible brilliance,
and that is a good way to die

1998

The Quiet Knight

The quiet knight forgets to swagger for the ladies
but the woman he loves becomes a queen
in the throne room of his chest and arms
and he never leaves
all the laundry or birth control to her

The quiet knight is the friend
of her body in bed and knows its secrets
and out of bed, he is her friend
and keeps her secrets

The quiet knight has no bellow or bravado
He has seen the innocents thrown in the mud
under the hooves of the galloping gallants
He has given them a ride to the shelter

The quiet knight does not insist on leading battle
But it is the quiet knight who holds the ground
and sticks around, when the flashbulbs have dimmed,
to help the wounded home,

after bringing to them, in his cupped hands,
a drink of his courage and nobility

1998

The Woman Dear to Herself
(Azizatu Nafsiha)

The woman dear to herself lives in the heart,
alive to the everywhere presence of divinity
The woman dear to herself does not lose herself
in the presence of man,
woman, or child

The woman dear to herself loves
for another what she loves for herself,
and loves for herself,
neither in conquest nor in surrender

In love she remains whole
She doesn't chop herself like an onion
She doesn't peel herself and sweep away the dry peelings

The woman dear to herself, when she has her period,
says "I have my period,"
understanding that her powers are not a curse
She knows the geography of her body
and how to give good directions home
to those whom she selects for company

The woman dear to herself
gives herself breast exams and running shoes
and eats well and washes her face in the river
and cherishes the beauty in other women as in her self
She wears dignity like a mantle
It swings lightly from her shoulders when she moves

The woman dear to herself, when come the spring rains
—O meeting with the beloved!—
knows where to find the first stalks of green

So that when the rivulets stream and stream
over brown muds, crocuses will open oval buds and hyacinths
will triumph flush and pink tiny flower after tiny flower and
    jonquils
everywhere
        delight
                the woman dear to herself,
she who lives
in the heart
of every man,
woman, and child

1996

To My Queenly Daughters

My little daughters, walk beside me
One day we will walk shoulder to shoulder,
three queens, gracious and savage,
coming from the World's Beginning,
neither of the East nor of the West, we,
but luminous. So tune your antennae.

And guard your secrets,
O my little daughters who will one day be queens
And open your treasure chests. Know what you have,
pearls and scorpions. I am arming you
with talismans, the talon of the falcon I was.
"Because I love you" is a good answer
to nearly everything you will ask me
so remember it when I am gone.

Hold my hands, my daughters. And we will burn grandly,
like oil lamps in the niches of the Grand Mosque
And we will signal to the Pleiades
and the outer planets, our friends and allies
full of grace and savagery,
It is time, come now, it is time

2000

My Body Is Not Your Battleground

My body is not your battleground
My breasts are neither wells nor mountains,
neither Badr nor Uhud
My breasts do not want to lead revolutions
nor to become prisoners of war
My breasts seek amnesty; release them
so I can glory in their milktipped fullness,
so I can offer them to my sweet love
without your flags and banners on them

My body is not your battleground
My hair is neither sacred nor cheap,
neither the cause of your disarray
nor the path to your liberation
My hair will not bring progress and clean water
if it flies unbraided in the breeze
It will not save us from our attackers
if it is wrapped and shielded from the sun
Untangle your hands from my hair
so I can comb and delight in it,
so I can honor and anoint it,
so I can spill it over the chest of my sweet love

My body is not your battleground
My private garden is not your tillage
My thighs are not highways to your Golden City
My belly is not the store of your bushels of wheat
My womb is not the cradle of your soldiers,
not the ship of your journey to the homeland
Leave me to discover the lakes
that glisten in my green forests
and to understand the power of their waters

Leave me to fill or not fill my chalice
with the wine or honey of my sweet love
Is it your skin that will tear
when the head of the new world emerges?

My body is not your battleground
How dare you put your hand
where I have not given permission
Has God, then, given you permission
to put your hand there?
My body is not your battleground
Withdraw from the eastern fronts and the western
Withdraw these armaments and this siege
so that I may prepare the earth
for the new age of lilac and clover,
so that I may celebrate this spring
the pageant of beauty with my sweet love

1998

Sacred Immorality

You smashed my pottery
One day I began to glue it back together
and for that
you said I was a liar and a cheat

You took away my beauty
When I began to wipe off ugliness
You called it vanity
and said I looked like women of the street

You cut my guitar strings
When I pulled my own hairs off my head
so I could hear a few notes of redemptive grace,
you said my music was profanity

You say the devil is getting his hooks in me
I think the devil's hooks have been in me a very long time
Thank God I'm pulling from my flesh
this satanic holiness
and inhaling, with every breath,
the oxygen of sacred immorality

1998

Men Kill Me

Men kill me
How they think the sun is all for them
and the water is all for them
How they accept the wind at their backs
as if the wind was the handmaid of their father
and they inherited her without a murmur

Men kill me
How they think the earth of green and gold and God
    is all for them
How they feel generous in leaving one small spot
between four walls for all the women of the world
How they swallow all the meadows' wild color upon color
and feel grand if they remember to bring
    one red rose for a woman

Men kill me
How, if a woman takes one ray of the sun
or cuts a river through the water,
they accuse her of violating
the Copernican order,
of upsetting the orbits of the planets
and the orbits of the pilgrims at the Ka'ba

Men kill me
How they forget that the world is resting
on the back of a tortoise
and the tortoise is poised on a spider
and the spider is dangling like a drop of sweat
from the temple of the woman scrubbing the floor
under the feet of Copernicus and the pilgrims at the Ka'ba

1998

Ishtar Awakens in Chicago

My arrogance knows no bounds
and I will make no peace today,
and you should be so lucky
to find a woman like me

Today I crawled out of the human pit
and am covered with lice
Today I flayed myself of my skin
and am raw like a serrated wound,
and you should be so lucky

Today neither will the East claim me
nor the West admit me
Today my belly is a well
wherein serpents are coiled
ready to poison the world,
and you should be so lucky

Today the cities of the North
want to grind me into insta-woman
soluble in their drinking water
And the Southern smalltowns
want to lynch each of my breasts
for a different crime
and gag each of my mouths
with a different dead flower

All I have is my arrogance
I will teach it to lean back
and smoke a cigarette in your faces,
and you should be so lucky

No, I will make no peace
even though my hands are empty
No, I will cut off my breast
and slit the throat of my child
and lap up poison with my tongue
before I make peace with you today

Today I talk big
Did you think all the big talk
was for you?
Did you think the big death
and the big love
was the world's big gift to you?

I will talk as big as I please
I will be all or nothing
And I will jump before the heavy trucks
And I will saw off my leg at the thigh
before I bend one womanly knee

I am poison
and you will drink me
And you should be so lucky

1998

Thawrah des Odalisques at the Matisse Retrospective

Yawm min al-ayyam we just decided: Enough is enough
A unique opportunity, the Retrospective brought us all together
I looked across the gallery at Red Culottes and gave the signal
She passed it on to Woman in Veil and we kicked
    through canvas
Most of us have very good legs—lower body strength,
    you know
The Persian Model needed help, but it wasn't her,
it was the way she was drawn

    Mais it wasn't just one day we up and decided, *CulottesGris,*
    I have to disagree. *Je voudrais dire*
    c'etais les deux Mauresques muhajabas

Hey, we don't know they were Moroccan, With Magnolias

    Oui, mais it was like seeing *nous-mêmes,*
    Mauresque comme moi, models of ourselves, walk by in veils
    then walk coolly out of the museum

"She must be so uncomfortable in that position"
these two museumgoers murmured in front of Two Odalisques
Suddenly I felt my back aching
a seventy-five year kind of ache
I scattered the chessboard I had been painted with

We woke up Harmony in Yellow
(all she'd eaten in years was lemons)
Asia and Zulma, older, led the procession
"Everyone whose arms are numb from sleeping on them,
    raise your hands"
Blue Nude decided she was with us
    because of her eyes and her posture

Pink Nude wanted in though she wasn't an odalisque
because "that bastard, my ass is cold from these blue tiles
and I can't love a man who made my head smaller than my tits,
almost an afterthought"
Being very Modern she knew all
the dirty words in several languages
and was great fun to have along
Woman with Goldfish came
She had a migraine, *miskini*, from all those years
sitting and staring at her goldfish swim in circles
around, around, around, around,
till fish was woman and woman fish
She brought the goldfish, bowl and all, under her arm
We shook the others by the ostrich feather hats,
knocked on the Renoirs next door
    to see if they wanted to come
but they still believed the hype, were getting lots of praise
as the Impressionists' girls, people came from miles around,
    that type of thing
We didn't judge them, what woman doesn't like attention?

Awwal shee we all wanted to pee
Then Hindu Pose and With Tambourine
    led us in some stretches
I helped With Turkish Chair rebraid her hair
Most of the Culottes and With Magnolias wanted clothes
Their nipples were icy and they were coughing,
the draft in the gallery had gone straight to their chests
The next thing everybody wanted to do was leave
The guards were understandably upset but we noticed
many of us were larger than life

tara nahna akbar minhum
'w akbar min abuhum!
Zulma reached up for us being tallest
and tore down museum banners
 for the ones who wanted clothes
Somebody must have called the Board Members,
 because outside
men with distinguished looks and women with perfect makeup
and large expensive brooches tried to reason with us
Somehow the news leaked quickly to the press

Pink Nude got the most movie offers
Playboy tried to talk the pants off the Culottes
Vantage offered a lucrative advance to With Magnolias
 for a book deal
with promos on *Good Morning America,*
 and Geraldo wanted to know
did Matisse ever masturbate with us.
 Matisse this, Matisse that—
No one wanted to know about us

Statements were issued on our behalf
by Arab nationalists, Iranian dissidents, Western feminists
The National Organization for Women got annoyed
after some of us put on *hijab,*
and wouldn't let us speak at their rally,
but wanted us up on their dais as tokens of diversity
Then someone spread conspiracy rumors about us
 among the Arabs
Like, why had we hung around so long? In the capitals
of the Western world so long? With our legs so open?
You can see *les implications dangereuses*
It did no good to tell them we didn't choose the poses
we were painted in. Or that anyway, our sexuality,

when we choose to put it into play,
is our business. Narrow-minded bastards,
I'll say it even though they are my Arab brothers,
a hundred years since we entered those paintings
and they're still stuck in a Neanderthal cave
on that whole man-woman thing.

The world we woke to is full of countries
most of us have never heard of before:
The Ottomans had fallen in 1924. Twenty-two
Arab states and Israel
in the middle like a stiletto.
The Lamé Robe immediately got involved
in the Algerian civil war. She had family
alive, on different sides.
The Persian Model went on Hajj, got arrested
in an anti-Saudi demonstration (oh those Iranians)
Red Culottes, it turned out, had cancer
Exposure of the breasts to Paris and New York air
Zulm wallah, so that was when
I, Small Odalisque in a Purple Robe,
decided to study law, all of it:
English Common, Napoleonic Code,
German, Russian, Turkish, Egyptian civil,
Islamic shariah, American constitutional, one by one
We sued the pants off the Matisse estate and the museums:
Cruel and unusual contortions, unhealthy and unfair
working conditions at nonexistent wages,
in many cases with only lemons and oranges to eat,
causing citric overdosage and extreme
puckering,

all to indulge somebody's sense of color. Pink Nude
was there to say, fuck your sense of color

in the twenty-seven European languages
she'd overheard from sixty years of patrons,
which the jury was instructed to disregard

I in my Purple Robe gave the closing argument
"We're not anti-art, we love the Expressionists.
And the Impressionists, and Cubists even. Why,
just last week, I bought a Klimt.
Even Matisse, we love his cutouts,
pure color, pure shape set free in modern space.
We just don't want to be made something we're not
It's a lie. The paintings lie about us. We were made to live a lie."
The post–Cold War jury was sympathetic
We were starting to make headway and it felt good

Suddenly Asia got a call
    from Bayadère Culottes wanting to end it,
sobbing, "we don't fit in anywhere anymore it's too late too late,
with Matisse we are nothing, without Matisse nothing.
You can take the odalisque out of the oda, but can you ever
take the oda out of the odalisque, can you can you?"
Harmony in Yellow said we had to get back together
    awwal b'awwal
Maybe form a support group, as in
"Hi I'm Odalisque with Big Breasts.
I was painted by Matisse,
but I'm in control now."

That's when we found out With Magnolias
    had been painted pregnant
so we all got together for her delivery
She sat in an Ottoman-era birthing chair
we took out of a photograph
(I got to marveling at that—
how many things can we pull from history and reuse?)

We held her hands, Bayadère wiped her brow
We were all wondering *ya allah, ya fattah* but afraid
Would the baby be smothered by the same aesthetic forms,
would it be killed by paint fumes from another era
before it had a chance to breathe its options?
She screamed She pushed She crowned She gushed And then!

It was like nothing any of us had ever seen. Pure life,
    pure energy.
It was a girl! She waved her fists. She let go
with a high-pitched protest to the world.
Only a smudge
Only a tiny smudge, lime-green, on her left temple
I, Small Odalisque, drew up my purple robe and ululated
and we all ululated
in post-odalisquesque
jube-jube-jube-jube-jubilation

1994

If the Odalisques

If all the odalisques
in all the paintings
in all the museums
in all the capitals of Europe
got up and left,
they'd leave a big hole in the wall
and people who'd come to stare through it
'd get sucked into Asia and Africa
until the whole peninsula of Europe
'd disappear between those two great
thighs of the world

1994

Copulation in English

We are going to dip English backward
by its Shakespearean tresses
arcing its spine like a crescent
We are going to rewrite English in Arabic

— يـا عين , يـا عين —

and all the languages of our blood
We are going to give English the makeover of its lifetime,
darkening the rims of its eyes with Hindi antimony,
making it blush Farsi roses

— لــيل لـيلـي لـيل لـيلـي لـيل لـيلـي لـيلا —

We are going to make English dizzy
until English vomits its history,
Norman, Saxon, Celtic, down
to its Druid dregs
We won't stop playing with English
We are the new bullies in the schoolyard
and we like the merry-go-round of nouns and adjectives
and onomatopoetics and objective correlatives

We will bewilder English in the Aramaic of Jesus

الوهيم الوهيم . . . الهي الهي , لما شفقتني

We know its biblical heart better than it knows itself
and hold the blades of these lilies-of-the-valley
against its jugular vein

We are going to make English love us
and kiss us and explore us with its tongues
Then we will play hard-to-get
and English will have to phone
and leave message after message of desire on our machines
English will have to learn what to say to please us:

تذ للــت , تــذ لّـت حـتى رق لـي قلـب حاسـدي

English has never tasted anything this purple,
seen mangos this bursting, trickling down its poems,
pomegranates spraying the tart red seeds
over its stories like white linen
English has never smelled cardamom this ecstatic
or breathed rhetoric this thick with love

English will come to us hoarse with the passion
we will have taught English to have
and English will never be the same and will never regret us
Although, after this night of intense copulation,
we may slaughter English in its bed and redeem our honor,
even while pregnant with English's bastard
و إذا الـــفجـــر مطلُ كـالحـــريق

1997

The Pistols of Emir Abdel Qader

Dec. 11, 1997: "Saddam executes 800 political prisoners
in the last two weeks"

—Iraqi Broadcasting Corporation, London.

Mar. 28, 1998: "One million Iraqis have left Iraq and scattered
to the farthest limits of the earth in recent years—this is
our harvest from war and sanctions."

—Iraqi dissident

The grandfather of your grandfather
fled his Algeria when the French
invaded it, emptying its cities,
battering the sides of its mountains with bullets
The people bled and tumbled down the mountainsides
The ones who emigrate tell only half the story

That is why we keep ready
the pistols of Emir Abdel Qader

Your mother is not a real
Damascene. She has other people
who would recognize her great-grandfather's green eyes
if they saw her, would embrace her, take her back
to their village to marry one of their sons
Being an immigrant means always having other people

That is why we wear white
and keep ready the pistols
of Emir Abdel Qader

You see the rockbruised body, the one
unheeded at the foot of a mountain in Algeria
or among the eight hundred dead in Babylon today?
That body could have become the father

or the mother of a girl like you
The ones we left behind have the other half of our story

That is why we trill with our tongues
and keep ready the pistols
of Emir Abdel Qader

We may have left Algeria a hundred years ago
or fled the ruins of Babylon yesterday,
but we never left the rockbruised body
unheeded at the foot of the mountain
We carried it with us. We carry it with us.
That is the meaning of the bruise on your heart

That is why
we wear white
and trill with our tongues
and holster the pistols
of Emir Abdel Qader

1997/1998

Disbeliever

On January 11, 1998, unidentified gunmen entered a movie theater
and a small mosque in Sidi Ahmed near Algiers and massacred
120 men, women, and children at close range during Algeria's
ongoing civil conflict.

By the limping of the people of Iraq
By the sound of frantic running in Qana, in Kosovo
By the men and boys of Hama massacred
By the swollen bodies in a river in Rwanda
and Afghani women and the writers of Algiers,
I am a disbeliever

in everything that refuses to kiss
full on the lips the ones still living
and receive them in the bosom of the self,
no matter the religion or the nation or the race
I am a disbeliever in everything
that does not say "How was the movie? I love you"

I need a body outside my life that can travel and kneel
on the sidewalk beside a movie theater in Algiers
over the bodies of the supple children
who will never be my children's playmates or marry them
over the bodies of the men and women
who will never write me a letter,
will never phone me from Algiers:
"How was the movie? I love you. I love you."

I need time outside this history
where I can whisper in the ear of each of them,
By God, you will never be forgotten
By God, I will make sure the world
buries its face in your beautiful hair,

sings to you, learns your name and your music,
lifts you up in the crook of its arm like a gift

I am a disbeliever
in everything but the purity of the bodies
of the men and women—with or without the veil,
with or without the markings of the right identity—
in everything but the suppleness of the children
I am a disbeliever in every scripture
in the world that leaves out
"How was the movie? I love you. I love you."

1998

Parturition 1999

In Iraq, after U.S. bombing,
depleted uranium, Saddam,
and sanctions,
people are having babies with no faces,
missing organs,
stumps for limbs,
no genitals

Everyone alive
is the mother

The father is a misshapen
beast who humps
the skin-and-bones body
while we watch, ashamed

Everyone in the world today
belongs to the age of deformity.
God too.

Here is an infant whose arms
are gelled to her torso in a tangled pulp,

the way we are all
flesh and veined together,
if we knew

No eyes or nose,
a sweet mouth:
How does God make such a thing?

The doctor is shuddering behind the door,
dreading the next delivery,
collecting pictures from Hiroshima on the Tigris

to enter on the record
of man's obscenities

1999

Snowfall on the Colossal Ruins

In the Roman amphitheater in Amman,
life is beautiful and sad. Unexpected snow
falls like a gift from heaven, settles
slowly on the hillocks,
curves, and rumps of bodies
strewn across the steps. The human floor
stirs. Thousands of Iraqis sleep here
nightly, this winter of the year 2000,
this tenth winter of the sanctions.
The proud, the dignified,
the ones you might have met in gracious homes
by appointment, bringing with you flowers,
fruit, or any small token,
to avoid arriving empty-handed,
you will find them here, roseate cheek
laid against the subzero stone.
You will find them curled against each other
in piles, so that a walker must step watchfully
not to tread on wrist or groin.
You will find minds trained
in the construction of buildings and poems
wrapped around a crate of unsold chewing gum.
You will find them here, parentless girls
and boys, who in former days
were carefully forbidden
to stay out past a certain hour.
You will find them here now, some ready
to sell to you for next to nothing
anything they still own,
snowflakes clinging
to their lush Iraqi lashes, a bare leg

here and there gleaming golden in moonlight.
There is not cover enough to go around
in the Roman coliseum in Amman.
You will find them here coughing
in the air of this winter, turning
from one side to the other, exposed
to whatever is to fall upon them next,
and not upon us, not tonight.

2000

Khidr's Riddle

It is a tiny hearing aid.
You will be able
to detect the sound
of grass growing, the thunder
of a thousand blades raised
under your foot.

It is a vial of eyedrops.
You will discern the epic
unfolding in every mote
of matter, the poem being written
and unwritten in every face.
Civilizations rise and fall,
whole species speak sagas
in that stone you kicked this morning.

It is a medicine.
Take it to perceive
worlds under the world, realities
cupped inside the belly
of reality.

It is a warning.
Your nerves will tentacle
across the globe. Rivers
will delta into your bloodstream.
The burbling liquids of Mars
will boil your medulla oblongata
and the rocks of Saturn's rings
will ice the base of your spine.

Joys, innumerable joys,
like the coming back of children

grown and bearing children,
each bearing baskets of harvest
berries, will fall into your lap.

It is a bucket into the well
of the world's soul.
Be careful. You will also
drink the pain of those you hate
and hear the last pleas
of the mad and butchered of the earth.

The wall of your back will crumble
under the weight of our heritage
of cruelty to each other.
The dam of your mercy will burst.
Consider: Will the flood ensuing drown
or irrigate, at last, the small field
you have been hoeing
in your heart?

2000

We Will Continue Like Twin Towers

Maybe they had never met before they flew
through the last air, the woman and the man
who held hands and leapt together
from the burning tower
of the World Trade Center.

Like the bride and groom of bombed Beirut
who walked across death-filled debris to marry,
even knowing that beneath their feet
everything that kills hope was being unleashed,
they held fast to the handclasp.

If the moon enters her darkest phases,
we will continue to walk the earth
making our own small light wherever we go
until her waxing time returns.

I will continue to invite your children
to play with my children.
Will you continue to want your children
to come and go with mine?

We will continue to walk the earth
carrying our small supplies of grace
We will continue to fly even now
that we have been so harshly reminded

of what we can never forget again:
That our lives have always been as fragile,
as dependent on each other, and as beautiful
as the flight of the woman and the man,

twin towers in my sight,
who jumped into the last air hand in hand

2001

The Fires Have Begun

There is a World Love Center inside my ribcage
There is a World Hate Center inside me too
The fires have begun. The fires have begun,
And I don't know which one
Is going to crumble first.

2001

Fatima Migrates in October

I am the birds of October,
the flocks of migration
I am the first woman in the new country
Who will dare love me?

I am Eve after Eden,
washing up on the shore at Jeddah,
the Crusoe of this island
I nurse Abel on one breast
and Cain on the other
and they are tearing me apart

I am Zainab after Karbala
I am the last shriek
of the last despair
of the last tribe of man on earth

I am Malinche in the age of Cortez
taking the conquistador to my bed,
making him father my new nation
that will smash his helmet one day

I am the women of the Oregon Trail,
burying men and children by the road
and continuing the journey in their names
I am Harriet parting the sea,
leading my people to freedom,

and Hagar scraping the sands,
shaking my fist at the angel,
wresting water from rock,
creating a new constellation in the sky
of human settlement

I deliver a new world
from between my immense thighs,
gasping, wriggling, slippery
with new blood

I enter history
and break its windows,
taking from its shelves
whatever pleases me:

This jar of blue face-paint from Nefertiti
This veil from the Queen of Sheba
This damascene steel dagger
from Shajarat al-Durr, the sultana
of ninety-nine violent nights

I take the hoarse desire of Zuleika
and the purity of Mary in her tower
I take the curses of Dido for Aeneas
and Cleopatra's poison asp,
for the heart is a betrayer

I take the reed basket of Moses' mother
I will not let Pharaoh kill the children
I take the wealth of Khadija
and the eloquence of Aisha
I take the laughter of Sakina in the city

and the lantern of Rabia in the desert
I take passion from Laila's breasts,
joy from Shireen's lips,
delight from the embroidered sleeves of Wallada
I take the lament from the throat of Khansaa

I am the last survivor of the massacre of Deir Yassin
and the last living descendent of the dead at Wounded Knee

I am the last to crawl out from under the rubble of corpses
I am looking for the new country
I am flying toward the outer sea

My world is in flames behind me
My world is this moment about to begin
I am the boiling blood of the heart
coming up from between the lips
I am a woman in her last desperation

and her first energy
I am Fatima
Do you dare love me?

1998

Redwoods

We are tired of your ancient language
When will you learn to speak new words?
Have you ever opened the book of the river?
The longest exile is exile of the heart
The only passage for return is love

We are sick of your outdated poetry,
beating its breast for the old palm trees
Your ancient palm oasis is not here but see,
the redwood trees have majesty and grace
and beneath them rivers flow

We don't believe in your seventh-century victories
or your ninth-century liturgies anymore
We are done with your tenth-century religion
We are tired of your gods
We do not like the gods that set

We are frightened by the wounds you carry
Why do you adorn us with them?
No one in this country understands grief
This blood you smear on our necks every morning
only brings the wolves to our throats

We no longer hate your ancient enemies
Your enemies' children have become our lovers
We are having their babies, haven't you heard?
Still you deny the revelation of the redwoods,
magnificent, underneath which rivers flow

1998

Poem to My Prodigal Brother

Little brother, I see you
crumpling the fail-safe faith map they gave us,
tossing it to the wind and hang-gliding
into the valley.
You are full of reverence
for god in the raw.

Stay inside the four walls
of religion, they told us. Obey,
obey, obey—obey what?
My body catching this wind is obeying
the pulse of the breathtaking Divine.
You, canoeing those rapids, are breaking
into the spray of larger, unseen Waves.

I don't know how to stop this unfolding
of limbs, this levitation of self into self.
I don't know much anymore.
It is time for us not to know.
We radiate light from our darkness.
Doubt, the kind I hear in you,
is a sign of restlessness for God.

All this being lost has more truth in it
than the pocket-watch faith of believers
who stay on dry ground,
never wetting the hem of their piety.
How is it faith if they never jump
off the ledge of the familiar?

Let's flip them the birdie and fly,
swim, rock climb, claw thorns
that puncture us like question marks.

Little brother, here's the one thing I know:
Our only outside chance at the sacred
comes through this being astray.

1998

Would That I Had Met You in Amman

Would that I had met you in Amman
Do you know that I have stood and waited
In the amphitheater since Roman times?
For a poet, for Khidr, for a woman or a man
For a music as well from heaven as from hell

Do you know that I have scraped the gate
Time after time and left the jasmine hanging
To pace the city Philadelphia, to scan
The skies and roads for—I don't know, a sign
Would that I had met you in Amman

I have been searching for a Canaanite
Or priest of Ur to take me by the hand
Through some unspeakable, disused ancient rite
Into the raw wound of a pagan truth
To believe or disbelieve with you, or god or man—
Would that I had met you in Amman

1998

Affirmative Action Sonnet

So you think I play the multiculture card
and sign up for affirmative action verse,
slide into print with poetry that's worse?
So you think I get excused from being good

by throwing in Third-World saffron and some veils?
Now is the summer of minority malcontent
They have no Idea of Order in the West—
But I do not insist on difference. Difference pales

beside the horrors facing our race
—the human one: hunger, HIV, genocide,
the unconscionable global marketplace
Where is the salve? We write. We recognize

—we must—each other in millennial glow
or we will die from what we do not know

That's all these smoke-and-mirror poems do
I came across the world to write for you

1998

Jasmine Snowfall

I.

Nizar, Nizar,
Mahmoud, Fadwa:
What is the shape of a family's
slow afternoon on a balcony,
the woman leaning low
to talk to a child in the street?
What is the scent of mint or a city?
What do the stones
of Jerusalem mean,
what is Beirut
and the sea?
Is there a replica at Epcot or Disney?
Can I watch it on MTV?

I am searching in O'Hare Airport
for anyone who can teach me
if Route 66 leads to Mecca
or to the abyss
I am looking down the concourse crowded
with the masses of Judgement Day
for a human or jinn who can tell me
how to board a homeward plane

II.

We are the children of '67,
sprung from between the cracks
of the last broken tile in the house
What is it like to have neighbors
who know you before you are born?
What is it like to have a grandmother

who waters the flowers like tribes,
a grandfather who grows by the side of your house
like a tree?

Born from the womb of an airplane,
we came out with a rush of jetstream
We ford the channels looking for a TV show
to fill an hour between Ramallah and the hole in our jeans
We light a cigarette of boredom
between "Unity, Freedom, Socialism"
and "Islam is the Solution"
We forage for an applecore to tide us over
between the bombing of Baghdad
and the last subway to the Lower East Side

III.

Does the world of white jasmine remember us?
I heard the gate scrape shut behind me,
the gate of language shutting the poetry
I move my lips but no words come in Arabic

Nizar, Badr, Nazek,
Samih, Buland, Abdulwahhab, Jabra,
Adonis, Etel, Ghada,
we are out here beyond
the last bus stop of your exile
Write to us sometime

IV.

No one here knows how to pronounce our names
Walt, how do you pronounce our names?
Emily, Carl, Langston, Hart,
Allen, Adrienne, Coleman, Sonya,
Amiri, Marge, Joy, Sandra,
how do you come to America?

I log on to the future but no e-mail arrives
There is no record of white jasmine in this listserv

V.

If you've never smelled clover or cardamom,
would you know the difference
between the well of a village and a wound in the breast?
between a Free Trade Zone and a genocidal siege?
between the Fijeh Spring waters
and the effect for generations to come
of radioactive Gulf War weapons
on children born in Iraq?

The flakes of a jasmine snowfall
gather softly in the fields,
gather on the iron balconies
of the Lower East Side

1998

The Fork in the Road

I.

To find the salve
for this wound you carry
without knowing its name,
you must return to the house
where you were born

in the old country. Go,
get to Damascus.
Find a way past the border
police. Enter through rock
if you must, cry open sesame.

You must find Baghdad Street.
Follow Baghdad Street
and follow and follow it
until you reach the main gate
of the Martyrs Cemetery.

That's the End of the Line,
where the trolley stopped, and behind it
is the land your grandfather farmed.
There he kept the Arabian mares.
Ask who remembers the Arabian mares.

Surely someone will remember the mares
and the man who traded them
until hard times and hard bread.
They say he found a treasure
that fire cannot eat.

Enter the crumbling houses.
Say: I was born here,

have you ever heard my name?
Have you heard of a treasure
that fire cannot eat?

II.

To find the grave of your lost brother
whose blood you carry,
you must stay in the new world
no matter what happens.
You must go into the vein

and heart of America. Go
into Indianapolis. After
the highway ends, follow the fields
of corn. Let a dirt road lead you
into a golden wooded world.

Sheridan, Shiloh. Tucked
between the shady farms is
a neat graveyard. Turn there, turn,
and turn again, like a braid.
Look for a small flat headstone.

Ask. Surely someone remembers
the little white coffin,
the boy with the blue
Mediterranean eyes,
the one we lost in the new world

and could not stop to find.
When you find him, the stone will turn
and there will be a cup
from which none else has drunk.
Say: This is my brother,

I have come to mark the place
where his cheeks sprouted

their delicate flowers.
Say: Who will drink
from this cup with me?

III.

Which do you want, choose.
You only get one journey.

1997

Learning to Pray All Over

One of these days, I'll add
A spiritual dimension to my life
One of these days I'll learn to pray
Here's how it will start: Alone
In a great jelly of time and space,
I will wallow in formlessness

At first. Never having tasted time
Outside the running from task to task,
I will drink my fill. Summer shade
And Popsicles beyond counting!
Nude I will go, everywhere, out-
rageous and inappropriate, reveling

Slowly I will begin to want
A rhythm to shape and space my days.
I will wake a little earlier. Eat
A little less. A little less will do,
Because I will be so still inside.
As still as the first daybreak.

Soon, like the second half of an eclipse,
The dark will shift. I'll come to know
That all this time I had been living
On a quarter of the light the real sun has.
That thing that trains and forces souls
to pray will move aside. I'll fall down,

as if blind, with my unused eyes. Groping,
I will discover the knobs and knots
In the wall of my own soul. Opening
Its door, I will emerge to fields

Of sorrows and wildflowers. I will find
Rock, stream, tree, wind, road

These, these will become my daily prayers.

2001

Glossary

Abdel Qader al-Jazairi ~ Algerian Sufi who found asylum in Damascus in the 1850s, after years of resisting French colonial takeover of Algeria.

Allahu akbar ~ Start of the call to prayer.

Avó ~ Grandmother (Portuguese).

Awwal b'awwal ~ First things first.

Awwal shee ~ First thing.

Badr and *Uhud* ~ The first battles fought by Muslims.

Ghayn, dād, khā ~ Letters in the Arabic alphabet.

Hijab ~ Common Muslim parlance for veiling.

Je voudrais dire c'etais les deux Mauresques muhajabas ~ I would like to say, it was the two veiled Moroccan women.

Joha ~ A wise fool in Middle Eastern folktales.

Khibbezé ~ A wild herb.

Khidr ~ Enigmatic wise man.

Khimar ~ Headscarf.

Kufi ~ Muslim yarmulke.

Mehndi ~ Henna, in India.

Miskini ~ Poor thing.

M'kayis ~ Bath attendant who scrubs bathers with a *kees* (a black abrasive bag).

Nous-mêmes, Mauresque comme moi ~ Ourselves, Moroccan like me.

O mãe ~ Mother (Portuguese).

Shaikhani ~ An Assyrian folkdance.

Shib-shibs ~ Flip-flops.

Shukran ~ Thank you.

Sirwal ~ Drawstring pants.

Tara nahna akbar minhum 'w akbar min abuhum ~ Say we're bigger'n they are 'n bigger'n their daddy.

Thawrah ~ revolution.

Ya allah, ya fattah - O opener of ways.

Yawm min al-ayyam - One day among days.

Yumma - Mother.

Zulm wallah - They did her wrong.

آمين - Amen.

يا عين , يا عين - How sweet, how sweet.

لــــيل لـيلـي لـيل لـيلـي لـيل لـيلـي لـيلا - The night, the night.

الوهيم الوهيم . . . الهي الهي , لما شفقتني - My Lord, my lord, why have you forsaken me?

تذ لـلـــت , تـــذ لـلـت حـتى رق لـي قلـب حاسـدي - Quote from a Sabah Fakhry song, "I humbled myself until even my enemy wept for me."

و إذا الـفجـر مطلُ كـالحـريق - Quote from an Um Kulthoum song, "Here comes the dawn upon us like a fire."

CONTEMPORARY POETRY SERIES
University of Central Florida

Mary Adams, *Epistles from the Planet Photosynthesis*
Diane Averill, *Branches Doubled Over with Fruit*
Tony Barnstone, *Impure*
Jennifer Bates, *The First Night Out of Eden*
George Bogin, *In a Surf of Strangers*
Van K. Brock, *The Hard Essential Landscape*
Jean Burden, *Taking Light from Each Other*
Lynn Butler, *Planting the Voice*
Cathleen Calbert, *Lessons in Space*
Daryl Ngee Chinn, *Soft Parts of the Back*
Robert Cooperman, *In the Household of Percy Bysshe Shelley*
Rebecca McClanahan Devet, *Mother Tongue*
Rebecca McClanahan Devet, *Mrs. Houdini*
Gerald Duff, *Calling Collect*
Malcolm Glass, *Bone Love*
Barbara L. Greenberg, *The Never-Not Sonnets*
Susan Hartman, *Dumb Show*
Lola Haskins, *Forty-four Ambitions for the Piano*
Lola Haskins, *Planting the Children*
William Hathaway, *Churlsgrace*
William Hathaway, *Looking into the Heart of Light*
Michael Hettich, *A Small Boat*
Ted Hirschfield, *Middle Mississippians: Encounters
    with the Prehistoric Amerindians*
Roald Hoffmann, *Gaps and Verges*
Roald Hoffmann, *The Metamict State*
Greg Johnson, *Aid and Comfort*
Markham Johnson, *Collecting the Light*
Mohja Kahf, *E-mails from Scheherazad*
Hannah Kahn, *Time, Wait*
Sharon Kraus, *Strange Land*
Susan McCaslin, *Flying Wounded*

Michael McFee, *Plain Air*

Judy Rowe Michaels, *The Forest of Wild Hands*

Richard Michelson, *Tap Dancing for the Relatives*

Judith Minty, *Dancing the Fault*

David Posner, *The Sandpipers*

Nicholas Rinaldi, *We Have Lost Our Fathers*

CarolAnn Russell, *The Red Envelope*

Don Schofield, *Approximately Paradise*

Penelope Schott, *Penelope: The Story of the Half-Scalped Woman*

Robert Siegel, *In a Pig's Eye*

Edmund Skellings, *Face Value*

Edmund Skellings, *Heart Attacks*

Floyd Skloot, *Music Appreciation*

Ron Smith, *Running Again in Hollywood Cemetery*

Susan Snively, *The Undertow*

Katherine Soniat, *Cracking Eggs*

Don Stap, *Letter at the End of Winter*

Joe Survant, *Rafting Rise*

Rawdon Tomlinson, *Deep Red*

Irene Willis, *They Tell Me You Danced*

Robley Wilson, *Everything Paid For*

John Woods, *Black Marigolds*

Mohja Kahf was born in Damascus, Syria, and came to the United States as a young child with her family. Now an associate professor at the University of Arkansas, she lives in the Ozarks with her husband and children. Kahf is a member of the Ozark Poets and Writers Collective and belongs to the Radius of Arab-American Writers, whose name she devised (its abbreviation, RAWI, means "storyteller" in Arabic). Kahf is a 2002 recipient of the Arkansas Arts Council Award for achievement in the literary arts.